OBSERVATION

# Observation

## PAUL CHENEOUR

Redgoldmusic.com

# Contents

*Dedication* vi

OBSERVATION

*About The Author* 29

Copyright © 2023 by Paul Cheneour

All rights reserved. No part of this book may be reproduced in any manner whatsoever without written permission except in the case of brief quotations embodied in critical articles and reviews.

First Printing, 2023

# Observation

Walk through this life
Offering
Courtesy
Kindness and
Consideration
Be the embodiment of love

Hidden deep within a human being
Is a longing to return to home
Another voice is also shouting
I want to be anywhere but here
What does this mean
Why do you run from your Self

Stop quarrelling and bickering
Take time to listen for a moment
Conflicts arise from beliefs
Insisting we are separate
On another level all is one
Be considerate
Especially towards yourself
Any system seeking to disempower
Is at odds with self-determination
And must be opposed

Actionist or reactionist
Are you a human
Reacting to influences
Or are you acting
From an inner knowing

Spiders and humans
Have much in common
Spiders weave their webs
How do they do this
Humans weave their webs
Why do they do this

We are drowning
In seas of information like junkies
Is there any wisdom or truth in it
What is seen today as true
Is derided as false tomorrow
We gorge at this trough
Like a herd of frenzied pigs
Lost in a terminal blindness

Hand burnt on a stove
And watched it heal
In only three weeks
The scar is a visible reminder
To beware
When dealing with fire

Returning to this country
Opened an understanding
Seeing with a fresh clarity
People damaged and broken
In body and spirit
Looking pale and crushed
Like ghosts
How did this happen

The music is slowly dying
Walking in this town
There is an air of despondency
A lingering apathy
That hangs like a dark cloud
Stop this nightmare
Cease this slavery
End this abuse
Say no to torture
Start the Music
Discover how to live
Like human beings again

This reality we create is our own
Every moment choices are made
Each one determining what is real
Begin exercising your choice muscle
That has laid dormant for years
Let go of negative programming
Begin unlearning
Choose to love yourselves
Then choose more wisely

The children looked
Sad old and defeated
I did not hear any laughter
I did not see any fun
What happened to them
Did you consent to this
The weight of insecurity
Is writ large on their faces
Who benefits
From this conformity
To misery

Do pylons
Standing in rows
In field
After field
After field
Get lonely


The Windscale nuclear disaster
Leaked dangerous radiation
Contaminating the countryside
Instead of admitting their responsibility
Authorities simply changed the name
From Windscale to Sellafield
Now there is no problem
Nothing to see here
Move along
Move along

A message
To all humans
It is time to
Wake up
Be aware that
Every being incarnated
Is seeking realisation

We are being assaulted
On all fronts now
There is a war on people
Populations are being poisoned
Media weaves their webs of lies
And a pandemic of deception
Bogus aid and free market conditions
Are only ploys to invade steal and
Decimate countries
Resist this onslaught
Anyway you can

If you choose to engage with me
There are consequences
Like the sun
My fire is warm and supportive
But be warned this fire
Will burn anyone to a cinder
If there is even a hint
Of deception

Look at time
What wristwatch would you choose
A Rolex
A Cartier
A Swatch
Is the quality of time any better
With an expensive mechanism
The choice of a time piece says more
About your attitude
And remember
Time is still an illusion

I was confronted by a hurtful accusation
Whilst working on a project
I am not your enemy I said
My comment cut through
The verbal onslaught
After a moment
Peace and calm were restored

Why be attached to difficulties
Carrying them like a thief in a swag bag
Perhaps they give comfort and purpose
But all they do is to keep you trapped
In what you think is your misfortune
If we could break out of this thought prison
We would shout for sheer joy
Now do you see
What is outside the bars in here

Elevating poverty to a noble state
Is to misunderstand the meaning
Of dying to your Self
When the personality surrenders
To the commanding soul
That alone is noble

Survival or extinction
Are the options we have before us
We can continue down the paths of
Avarice and greed
Ending in our destruction
Or we can become responsible
Share our abundance and survive
Which path
Will you choose

Flow like water
Follow the line of least resistance
It will move you in another direction
Why beat your head against a brick wall
Expecting the wall to break first

How long will it take
To value each individual
History is full of cruelties
People merely seen as
Units of production and consumption
As irritants to be controlled
To be organised
To be used
To Be abused
Cheated and punished
By some who would believe
They have a divine right to
Profit from population subjugation
The battle cry is growing louder
It is time to reclaim
Your rightful authority to be you

We humans are passionate beings
And that passion needs to be expressed
Real passion is the emotion most feared
And actively suppressed by those
Who would seek to control
What passes for real passion
Is often nothing more than anger and rage


Inequality between the rich and the poor
Exists only because of the belief
That inequality should continue to exist

What do I know
All I can say is
I do not know
But I know that
I do not know
But there is more to this knowing
And not knowing than meets the eye
It may take a life time or two
To really know
Of that
I have no doubt.

Suppression of female energy
Leads to conflict and misery
The masculine feminine balance
Needs to be restored
Within each of us
Then a peaceful humanity will emerge
As surely as daylight
Follows the dark of the night

When you humans thought
Differences could be solved
And peace restored
Up pops another crazy
And there we go again
Bombing
Bashing and
More bombing
With a bit more bombing
Thrown in for good measure
Blaming all and sundry
Like squabbling children
It is enough to make
The strongest among us
Weep with utter despair

Beware the words of mass deception
What do you know
What do you think you know
How do you know what you know
Are you speaking your truth
And what truth is that anyway
Can you tell truth from illusion
In this world of hype double speak and spin
Be careful with your own understanding
And although it may be dangerous
Ask questions
Ask more questions
And ask even more questions
Although it might end in incarceration
Keep your mind open
Do not be seduced
By manipulations or subterfuge
Be alert to fear and misdirection
What do you really know
Keep your wits about you
Become fully aware

In this summer of goodbyes
The girl blog from Iraq writes
It is not just physical goodbyes
That are hard to endure
It is the goodbyes to ourselves
To the collective loss of innocence
What have we allowed to happen
While sleepwalking
Pretending to be awake
This intense sadness
Is so overwhelming
It has remained with me for days

I will meet you round the bend
My friend
Where hearts can heal and souls
Can mend
Listen to the sound of eternity
Rippling through our lives
Like flowing water
In the shadow of the grand willow
Branches arms outstretched
Cradling us
In glorious compassion

No matter religious commercial or secular
Fundamentalists of all persuasions
Seek to bind and enslave
Reworking their dubious systems
Softly slipping their chains of servitude
Around vulnerable necks
Cast out their seductive temptations
Ignore their pleading calls
Steer your path away from
Dangerous entrapments

On the radio one morning
I heard a chilling definition of childhood
Saying that children are nothing more
Than a multi-disciplined experience
Blank objects or empty vassals
To be programmed and moulded
According to societal requirements
Or whatever is desired
My outrage at this callousness
Materialist thinking was incandescent
Children incarnate to fulfil their purpose
They are to be nurtured with kindness
Consideration and loving

Beware the desire for fame
Success brings pressures
Some visible
Most invisible
Failure allows a fresh start
Learning from previous mistakes
Look deep within yourself
And ask
Are you ready
For the trappings and tribulations
Of the fame and success you seek

Stop worrying
The universe is in perfect order
This one is at least or so we think
We humans are silly
Taking ourselves so seriously
Learning everything the hard way
Today be free and crazy
Play in the sand pit of your life

I was teaching a group of students
One of them admonished me to grow up
Stop being silly and crazy in our lessons
I have never had a discipline problem
Being childlike but not childish

Humans
Are both the problem
And the solution
Each one has a spirit soul
And a physical body
We make choices continuously
Choice making gives vitality
Outcomes flow from choices made
Do not judge those choices
Let them be what they are
Lose any guilt of right or wrong doing
Then choose again but choose differently
Now you are seeing
With eyes ears and heart

If your beliefs are rigid
An event will appear
To force a change
Allow attitudes to bend
Be open to soul needs
To all possibilities
And ask
What did I come here to do
Listen closely
An answer is riding on the wind
Heading towards you

Look at this world
With loving eyes
Be thankful for who you are
There is nothing
More serious than playing
Winning or losing
Does not matter
Enjoy the changing game
It is all an illusion anyway
See things for what they are
Not what they appear to be
Nor what you think
They ought to be

To talk with me
You do not need intelligence
Only another point of view
Rotate your views ninety degrees
Then another ninety
Now try multiple ways of looking
You might be surprised
At what you find

Money is a means of exchange
An enabler to be issued debt free
Do you want to know more about
The insane system you believe in
Do you
Do you
Are you ready
To let the ideology scales
Fall from your eyes and grasp
How big this fraudulent scam is
There is so much more to say
But I am not your teacher
I am just scattered smoke
A lone voice crying out
Lost in a whirlwind of ideas

Do you know who is running
This bizarre show called reality
The first step to discover any truth
Is to follow the money
Think sideways
Nothing is what it seems
When you go down
The rabbit hole of understanding

Creativity is being squeezed
From education
You must ask questions
When you find the right question
Within that question you will find
The seeds of your perfect answer

What is this reality thing anyway
Take a good look around
Not only with your eyes
But with your heart and soul
Then tell me what you think is real
This reality you believe in
Is there because you think it is there
Move beyond your conditioning
Open your heart
Now tell me what you see

Be grateful for who you are
Be the best person you can
Be true and honest with your Self
Manifesting flows from your thinking
Good bad and indifferent
Create a positive life
Leave limitation behind
The energy you give a thought
Is what you receive
Like the genie of the lamp says
Your wish is my command

Beware people selling a system of beliefs
If a dogma says you should fight an enemy and
If you are not with us then you are against us
Look for the terms of your enslavement
In the small print
Buyer should always beware

What is this
Not being good enough about
For whom are we not good enough
And how are we not good enough
These feelings of utter inadequacy
Come from a deep place buried within
And fed by unrealisable expectations
Detach from this negativity
Cease to operate from this perspective
Look into the centre of your being
Tell me how true this is for you

Cycles form from desire
And end in manifestation
A process of beginnings
And completions
Through many existences
Some short
Others are over eons
This is a time to open
And walk through
A new door

Use time wisely
The more time you have
The less you value it
The less time you have
The more you value it

Problems between people
Stem from dishonouring the Self
The world you experience
Is full of people who betray the Self
Resolution can only be experienced
If you see the victim or victimizer as other
Both are betraying the Self
And seeking the Self through the other
Both are calling out to each other
When that answer is heard
It is with conviction
And thanks to each other
Each is given a call to wake up
Only when they look deeply
Are both shown their own betrayal
What they will see
Is the other
In each other

I see a mirror
Showing me what I believe
Everything that happens
Is a reflection of
Some belief
I have about myself

A prayer of forgiveness
Admit fears and judgments
Ask to be strengthened
Ask to see beyond preconceptions
Ask to be open to truth
Ask to learn lessons from situations
Ask for guidance
Ask for support
Ask for relief from suffering
Ask for the highest good for all
Then be quiet
Your heart is now open

You will stay in pain
Until you turn to the abuser
And say this is unacceptable
I want you to stop right now
Then turn to yourself and ask
What can I learn from this pain

Be the window
Through which light passes
Not the object
That blocks it

Fairness is balance
Give what you have
Take what you need
Establish balance
Personally and materially
Discard anger and resentment.

Inspiration
Equals
The drawing in
And outflowing
Of breath

Flex the creative muscle
Allow inspiration
To happen through feeling
Know that love and god
Are the same thing
You bring to the table
What you allow

Manifest what you want
Say no
To what you do not want
The complication is
Knowing what you want
Or even if you do know
You do not trust wanting it
Inspect those unconscious fears
Look beyond appearances
In this now
There is only breath and self

To offer a skill
Knowledge or understanding
Is a service
Learning is viewed merely
As a utility or commodity
No longer the foundation
Of a fully rounded
Human being

Each time a leader changes
Old ideas and attitudes
Are swept away
New thinking is established
In the old regime
The despot was tolerated
And we survived
By the rules of the game
Demarcation lines were drawn
In the sands of consciousness
Stomachs now rumble
With forebodings
Will the little freedoms prized
From those rulers be lost
Can we survive this new change

Are you being desensitized
There is a numbing and brutalisation
Taking place
No matter the shade of administration
It needs your complicit conditioning
What else
Is being prepared for you

Here but not here
A feeling of being here
And not being here
But simply of the body
Watching
Floating
Observing
Restful and restless
Moving forward
Standing still
Heavy and light
These paradoxical feelings are curious
Something seems to be happening
Perhaps a change is taking place

Stand still for a moment
Examine your existence
Move within
Switch your lights on
Your life is your greatest gift
Do no waste it
Be in it
But not of it
Do not worry about failures

Leave a relationship
If you are being measured
Against an insurmountable
Yardstick

Being in the middle
Between alpha and omega
Confronted by dualism
Wanting to do things
And not wanting to do things
In equal measure
Is a strange sensation

An excruciating ouch
Woke me suddenly
I bit my tongue
It really hurt
How crazy is that

Work together
Co-operation is better
Than competition
So simple
But so true

We are living in turbulent times
Old establishments are creaking
And crumbing
Some may protest
But new structures will be more humane
Who would have thought when mankind
Was engaged in fierce bickering
Over climate or no climate change
A microscopic virus could achieve
So much so quickly

Crisis fans the flames of fear
Liberating us from outmoded ideas
Perhaps there is an opportunity to create
A fair equitable and just system
Only time will tell if humanity can rise
To this glorious possible occasion

Britain has officially left the European Union
We are sort of celebrating new year 2021
We are being told
This new year will be a year of hope
Life will be better than before
But here we stand full of scepticism
Quivering and shaking
In the cold light of day
The virus is becoming more virulent
Government responses more fatuous
And more inadequate
What to do

Observe with open eyes
Look and see clearly
Hear and listen to truth
What path
Will you
Follow

Paul Cheneour has walked a broader musical path throughout his career embracing European Classical, Jazz, Arab, Indian, Celtic, and other music's, culminating in his own 'World Fusion' style.

"Tapping into the source of creativity takes great courage and even greater competence in acquired skills.
Paul Cheneour, a leading UK jazz, classical and ethnic flautist/composer suffered a near fatal car crash in '91.

He recovered with the conviction that he needed to use his talent, life, and near-death experience to explore a new forms of creative expression. This amounts to an opening out to the influences available in the moment.

All the world's great musical and artistic traditions remain as resources and are no longer seen as restrictive boundaries"

(Interview extract by Michael Greevis for Colour Therapy Magazine UK. 1995)

www.ingramcontent.com/pod-product-compliance
Lightning Source LLC
Chambersburg PA
CBHW021134080526
44587CB00012B/1292